It's Not All
ANCIENT HISTORY

By Meish Goldish

Series Literacy Consultant
Dr Ros Fisher

Pearson Education Limited
Edinburgh Gate
Harlow
Essex CM20 2JE
England

www.longman.co.uk

ISBN 0 582 84138 0

Colour reproduction by Colourscan, Singapore
Printed and bound in China by Leo Paper Products Ltd.

The Publisher's policy is to use paper manufactured from sustainable forests.

The following people from **DK** have
contributed to the development of this product:

Art Director Rachael Foster

Martin Wilson **Managing Art Editor**	**Managing Editor** Marie Greenwood
Wilfrid Wood **Design**	**Editorial** Julie Ferris, Selina Wood
Brenda Clynch **Picture Research**	**Production** Gordana Simakovic
Richard Czapnik, Andy Smith **Cover Design**	**DTP** David McDonald

Consultants Robert Rowland and Philip Wilkinson

Dorling Kindersley would like to thank: Peter Bull for original artwork; Lucy Heaver for editorial assistance; Rose Horridge, Gemma Woodward and Hayley Smith in the DK Picture Library; Johnny Pau for additional cover design work.

Picture Credits: AKG London: 21t. Alamy Images: Robert Harding World Imagery 14; Stockfolio 27t. Ancient Art & Architecture Collection: 26t. The Art Archive: 28bl; British Museum/Eileen Tweedy 3tl, 15tl; Museo Nazionale Terme Rome/Dagli Orti 19br; Turkish and Islamic Art Museum Istanbul/Dagli Orti 18tl. Bridgeman Art Library, London/New York: 8t, 9tc; Alinari 3bl, 22tc; Index 16tr; The Stapleton Collection 10cr. British Waterways: 13tr. Corbis: Archivo Iconografico, S.A. 24t; Ed Bock 4b; James Davis; Eye Ubiquitous 20t; Philip Gould 10br; George Hall 5br; Dave G. Houser 20b; Hulton-Deutsch Collection 25t; Gilbert Iundt; Pawel Libera 16l; Tim Page 26bl; Paul A. Souders 12cr; Maiman Rick/Sygma 26br; TempSport 3br, 22tr.DK Images: British Library 4t, 15br. Ecoscene: 29b. Empics Ltd: Witters 22cr. Getty Images: AFP 23t; Bruce Ayers 30; David R. Frazier 9cr; Mike Caldwell 18tr; Peter Pearson 8b; Rich LaSalle 11; Time Life Pictures 25b.Mary Evans Picture Library: 7t, 29t. Werner Forman Archive: Biblioteca Nacional, Madrid 23br; Statens Historiska Museum, Stockholm 19t. Ronald Grant Archive: 21b. Pa Photos: Toby Melville 5tr. Reuters: 7b. Photo Scala, Florence: 10tr. Swatch Ag: 18bl. Jacket: Corbis: Bettmann front bl; Tim Thompson front t. Werner Forman Archive: Biblioteca Nacional, Madrid back.

All other images: 🗗 Dorling Kindersley © 2004. For further information see www.dkimages.com
Dorling Kindersley Ltd., 80 Strand, London WC2R ORL

Contents

Making Connections to the Past

History is the story of our past. The past connects us to today. Looking at history reveals how our human society has changed over time, and how we have learned from and built upon ancient knowledge. We would not be here today if it weren't for the cultures, discoveries and events that came before us. Exploring history shows us how the world has come to its present state. Knowledge of the past also helps us make informed decisions about the future.

The earliest Chinese inscriptions were made on bone (above), bamboo or wood.

Our ability to communicate rapidly through technology is based on the discoveries made by ancient civilizations.

This book begins by exploring the reasons people migrated and formed communities in certain lands. By looking at early settlements, we will find out how ideas still common and goods still used today spread across the globe. We will also recognize how multicultural societies are created as people of different backgrounds come to live in the same area.

East London has a thriving community of immigrants from Bangladesh. Street signs are written in both English and Bengali.

Next we will explore important inventions and discoveries from all over the world. Looking at the inventions of the past helps us to appreciate them. It also inspires us to improve life by developing even better inventions.

Finally, this book will examine important historical events. We will explore why some great empires grew, then broke apart. We will also look at how military alliances help to protect some countries from outside threats. Examining these matters and others will help us recognize patterns of human behaviour.

NATO is a military alliance among the nations of the North Atlantic.

Understanding Migration and Settlement

There are several reasons for studying migration and settlement. First we learn about our own cultural backgrounds. We also learn the reasons why people migrated to specific places. Most important, however, by studying migration, we see patterns in human behaviour. Knowledge of these patterns helps us to appreciate common human experiences. It also helps us to prepare for the future.

Searching for Fertile Land

From ancient times to the present day, people have migrated to find lands that they could farm. One of the first places people settled in was the Fertile Crescent in the Middle East. Today this area includes parts of Israel, Syria, Lebanon, Iraq, Jordan, Iran and Kuwait. Migration and settlement began before 5000 BC and continued for 3,000 years. The region's rich soil allowed people to grow many crops.

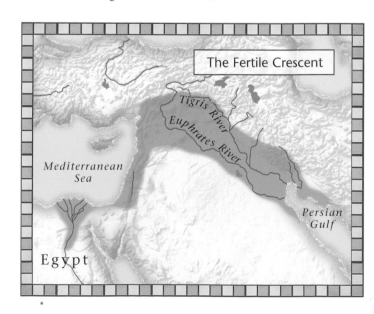

The Fertile Crescent

Tigris River
Euphrates River

Mediterranean Sea

Persian Gulf

Egypt

In more recent times, people from Ireland migrated in search of fertile farmland and a better life. In the early 1840s almost half of Ireland's population depended on potatoes for food and for income. Then in 1845 Ireland suffered a serious food shortage, or famine, because diseases struck the nation's potato crops. As a result, more than one million starving Irish people moved to the United States, Canada, Great Britain and Australia to seek work and a new life.

The journey across the Atlantic Ocean to North America in the mid-1800s could take between six and fourteen weeks. Conditions on the ships were very cramped.

This migration forever changed the cultures of these nations. For example, Irish people who migrated to the United States settled in and around Eastern cities because they lacked the money to travel further west. People who had been looking for suitable farmland were forced to accept the wages and working conditions offered to them in these cities. As a result, many of the Irish lived in poverty. This, as well as their customs and traditions, set them apart from some Americans. By the end of the 1800s there were more people of Irish origin in North America than in Ireland. The influence of Irish culture is still evident throughout North America today.

On 17th March every year, Irish Americans celebrate their heritage at St Patrick's Day parades.

Settling in Colonies

History shows that when people migrated to new lands, they tended to settle in colonies. These colonies often became independent nations. For example, in the 1600s, Britain formed the thirteen colonies in America to grow food and other raw materials to ship back to Europe. By 1776 the colonies had become an independent nation.

In 1620 the first European settlers, the Pilgrims, migrated from Great Britain to America by ship, on the *Mayflower*.

The United States has changed a great deal since the first colonies were established. It stretches from the Atlantic to the Pacific Ocean and is dotted with large cities such as Chicago, in Illinois.

In the early 1800s British prisons were overcrowded. Therefore, convicts were sent to Australia to live in penal colonies – distant settlements for criminals. In Australia, the convicts worked hard to farm the land and to build towns.

Convicts at the penal colony in Sydney, Australia

Today Sydney is a bustling city.

These past events have contributed to the cultural identity of the United States and Australia. They were both British colonies, and people continue to speak the English language in both nations.

Searching for Wealth

Another reason people migrate to a new area is to find wealth. The discovery of gold in the California hills in North America sparked a huge migration in the early 1850s. Gold-seeking adventurers from as far away as China, Chile and Australia rushed to California. People who realized that gold diggers needed food, shelter and other goods established businesses around them, forming towns and cities. The coming together of these cultures during the gold rush helps to explain why cities such as San Francisco have diverse populations today.

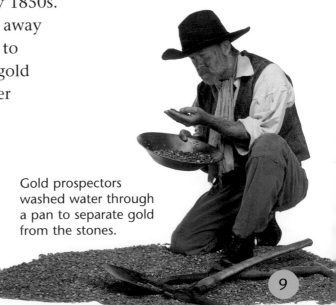

Gold prospectors washed water through a pan to separate gold from the stones.

9

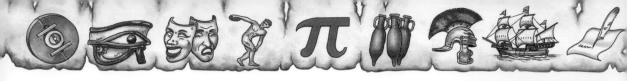

Migration for Trade

Trading food and materials was an important reason people throughout history migrated to new lands. For example, Egypt was one of the richest countries in ancient times. From about 3200 BC, Egyptians traded valuable items with other African and Middle Eastern civilizations. Egyptian merchants received such goods as timber, leopard skins and elephant tusks. Many Egyptians settled in these other areas to benefit from the trading industry.

These pottery jars were shaped to be packed tightly in a Roman merchant's ship.

Widespread trading sparked migration in ancient Rome. Roman ships carried olive oil, wine and other goods to distant ports in Britain and Germany. Returning ships brought food and raw materials to Italy. To maintain this thriving trade, some Romans established homes and businesses in these distant places.

Trade continued to inspire migration in more recent centuries. In the early 1600s, French fur traders travelled to North America to trade with Aboriginal Canadians. The trading businesses soon led to a permanent French settlement in Canada. French-speaking people still make up a part of Canada's population today.

Aboriginal Canadians trading with French explorers

Many signs in Canada are written in both French and English.

Effects of Migration

Today people continue to migrate to other countries for economic and political reasons. During the 1990s, about 120 million people lived or worked outside their native countries. There are both positive and negative effects of such migration. As people move from place to place, they bring their ideas and goods with them. They exchange these ideas and products with the peoples who have already settled in the area. This helps to create multicultural societies. It also builds respect and tolerance among different cultures.

The challenges of migration include increased demand for housing and health care, and lack of jobs for immigrants. As a result, many governments limit the number of people who can migrate to a country each year. Often, new culture groups clash with those that have already settled in an area. This causes tension until people learn to live together peacefully.

Chinatown in New York City, United States, has a large population of Chinese immigrants.

Conclusion

Migration to new lands will continue as long as people seek a better life. If we study the history of migration, we can learn about our ancestors and our own cultural identity. We can also learn important lessons from the past and develop a greater understanding of immigrant communities today.

Inventions and Discoveries

When we use a computer or watch a film, we don't think much about ancient history. However, discoveries made in the past enable us to enjoy many of today's activities. Without the inventions of early civilizations, there would be no houses, roads, medicines, games or even languages as we know them.

Buildings, Waterways and Roads

We often take our houses, schools and shops for granted. However, we owe many ancient cultures for these buildings. For example, the Native Americans of Mexico and the south western United States have built homes with adobe for more than 1,000 years. Adobe is made of mud, water and straw, and is pressed into blocks. The desert dwellers knew that adobe was a long-lasting building material that keeps a home cool, despite scorching temperatures outside.

Simple drills were used by ancient civilizations such as the Egyptians. The modern drill is powered by electricity, but uses a similar revolving motion.

Today, some homes are still made from adobe bricks. Adobe houses stay cooler than insulated homes.

The ancient Romans also built sturdy houses. Their plumbing skills were so advanced that many large Roman homes had their own water supplies. Today, we take indoor plumbing for granted, but it was the ancient Romans who developed the idea.

This rotating boat lift in Scotland lifts boats from a canal to an aqueduct 24 metres above.

The Romans also constructed aqueducts that carried water through long channels to cities and towns. People filled jugs with the water they needed from the public fountains. Amazingly, some of the old Roman aqueducts are still in use. Today, there are modern aqueducts in many countries. For example, the 37-metre-tall Pontcysyllte Aqueduct in Wales carries a whole canal across a river.

This is part of the famous Pont du Gard aqueduct in France, built by the ancient Romans. It was 50 kilometres long and carried large amounts of water daily to the city of Nîmes.

13

There is an old saying that "All roads lead to Rome." Rome was once the most important city in the world, and ancient Romans taught the modern world a great deal about building roads. The early Romans built an elaborate network of roads to connect Rome to regions under its control. Some of these roads stretched to distant cities in Europe and the Middle East.

The Romans used sound principles to build their roads. In fact, builders today use ancient Roman rules to construct new roads. Also, many modern roads in Europe still follow the same routes that the Romans travelled thousands of years ago.

The Appian Way is the most famous road built by the ancient Romans. It was constructed as a military highway more than 2,000 years ago. The Appian Way was originally 212 kilometres long and started in Rome. Later, the road was extended another 376 kilometres. Parts of the Appian Way are still used today.

the Appian Way

Roman Road Rules

Roman rules for road building still apply today.

- Use several layers of material, including dirt on the bottom and a hard surface on the top.

- Raise the road so water runs off the road into ditches.

- Try to make roads follow as straight a path as possible.

Science and Technology

It's hard to imagine a world without bicycles, cars and planes. Yet, we use them only because sometime between 5500 and 3000 BC someone invented the wheel. Archaeologists believe that the invention was probably created in Mesopotamia (present-day Iraq) or Asia. Although we are not exactly sure of when, where or how it happened, everyone agrees that the wheel is one of the most important inventions in human history. It is a perfect example of how ancient history is relevant to today's world.

Imagine what life would be like without books, magazines and newpapers. Again, we have ancient cultures to thank for inventing paper. Ancient Egyptians made paper from a plant called papyrus. They cut its stalks into thin slices and pressed them into sheets for writing. In AD 100 the ancient Chinese introduced papermaking techniques that are more like the ones we use today. They made paper from silk, and later from hemp, bark and bamboo.

The Sumerians used wheeled chariots to transport their soldiers. Today aerodynamic wheels help cyclists reach high speeds.

Early Chinese books were handwritten on paper. This book is about 1,000 years old.

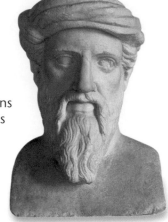

Pythagoras made important contributions to music, mathematics and astronomy.

Today's world of advanced technology, architecture and engineering owes a great deal to the mathematicians and scientists of long ago. Pythagoras, a Greek mathematician, lived around 550 BC. He developed a theory based on number patterns. Engineers, architects and car makers are just some of the people today who rely on Pythagoras's number patterns for their work.

Archimedes was a brilliant Greek scientist. He developed laws of physics that led to the invention of machines that could lift heavy objects such as the pulley. Without the machines based on Archimedes's ideas, modern-day construction would be virtually impossible.

Archimedes's laws of physics are used on modern-day building sites.

In today's world, we go to the doctor when we are sick. We trust doctors to know a great deal about the human body and about medicine. Much of that knowledge is based on discoveries made by ancient Greek and Roman doctors.

Aspirin has the same main ingredient as willow bark, an ancient remedy for pain.

Hippocrates was known as the "Father of Medicine". He lived 2,400 years ago. He and his followers wrote more than sixty medical books about diseases and injuries. Doctors today still recommend the rules of good health that Hippocrates introduced such as eating well, exercising and getting fresh air.

The ancient Chinese also contributed to the field of medicine, as did many Native American people. Much of Chinese and Native American medicine is based on using natural herbs and plants to heal the body. Some herbal remedies have made their way into modern medicine. For example, the Cherokee people long used the bark of the willow tree to treat fevers. The active ingredient in willow bark is salicylic acid – the main ingredient in aspirin.

The Hippocratic Oath

Hippocrates began a medical school. He made his students follow strict rules known as the Hippocratic Oath. New doctors swore to keep information between a patient and a doctor private, and to never harm a patient on purpose. Today doctors still take a version of the Hippocratic Oath before practising medicine.

Traces of ancient Arabic words can be found in many modern languages.

Ancient Roman capital letters, shown here, serve as the model for Roman-style lettering today.

Language

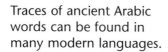

Roman numerals still appear on some clocks and watches.

Whom do we owe for the language that we speak, write and read? Many modern-day words and languages have their roots in ancient cultures. Latin, the language of the Roman empire, is not spoken any more. However, the twenty-six letters of the Roman alphabet are used in many languages, including English.

Thousands of English words contain Latin and Greek roots, including most scientific and medical terms.

Other English words have their roots in other early languages such as Anglo-Saxon and Norse.

Some English words reflect the religious beliefs of ancient peoples. The Vikings, for example, worshipped many different gods and goddesses. Their main god was Odin, or Woden. The day of the week named in his honour was Woden's-day. Over time, that name changed to the name we use – Wednesday. Similarly, the Norse god of thunder, Thor, had a different day named for him – Thor's-day, or Thursday.

Some of the names of our months also stem from ancient religions. The Roman god Janus, for example, was in charge of doorways and beginnings. January, the first month of the year, is named after him.

This 12th-century Viking tapestry shows one-eyed Odin (left) carrying an axe.

June was named after Juno, the Roman goddess of women.

Discovering the Roots

zero from the Arabic word *sifr*, meaning "empty"

acrobat from the Greek word *acros*, meaning "at the top of"

dinosaur from the Greek words *deinos*, meaning "fearful", and *sauros*, meaning "lizard"

ugly from the old Icelandic word *uggr*, meaning "fear"

pyjamas from the Persian words *pai*, meaning "leg", and *jama*, meaning "garment"

Religion

Just as modern languages developed from ancient civilizations, so did modern religious beliefs. Some of today's most prevalent religions are thousands of years old. For example, Hinduism developed in India approximately 4,000 years ago. Hindus believe that people should do good work and be honest with others. Similarly, Buddhism, founded in India some 2,500 years ago, teaches the value of respect for all living things.

This Christian church in Reykjavik, Iceland, was built in the 20th century.

The Jewish faith developed over 3,000 years ago. It introduced the idea of a single, all-powerful creator. Islam, revealed to the prophet Muhammad, also holds the belief in a single creator, Allah. Christianity follows the teachings of Jesus, born about 2,000 years ago. He taught the importance of loving all human beings. Today, Hindus, Buddhists, Jews, Muslims and Christians around the world still follow the beliefs of these ancient religions.

The Hindu temples at Angkor Wat in Cambodia were built between the 8th and the 13th centuries.

Sports and Entertainment

Since ancient times, storytelling has been a popular form of entertainment. Early people created myths to explain events in nature, such as thunder and sunrises. Often the characters in myths had superhuman powers. Many stories today feature superheroes in much the same way.

The ancient Greek theatre at Epidauros still stands.

People of different cultures often participated in or watched performances as a source of entertainment. The ancient Greeks made theatre a popular form of entertainment. By 400 BC actors were performing comedies and tragedies on stages throughout ancient Greece.

The Greeks were the first to use ampitheatre-style seating. These theatres were semi-circular with three main sections. The audience sat in curved rows of seats to watch a performance, and the theatres were in the open air. The walls of some early Greek theatres still stand today.

Stories about characters with superhuman powers, such as Spider-Man, are popular today.

Just as modern theatre has its roots in ancient Greek civilization, so does one of today's most popular athletic competitions: the Olympics. Over 2,700 years ago the Olympic Games were created as a way to honour the god Zeus. They were held every four years in Olympia. Events included discus and javelin throwing, boxing, wrestling, running and jumping. These events are also part of the modern Olympic Games.

Many of the events in the modern Olympics, such as discus throwing, took place in the ancient games.

After being abandoned for more than 1,500 years, the Olympic Games began again in Athens, Greece, in 1896. Different cities now compete to host the games. Today, the Olympic Games bring athletes and spectators from around the world together for two weeks to celebrate the spirit of sportsmanship.

Conclusion

The next time you turn on the water, visit the doctor or go to the cinema, think about the past. One important purpose of looking at the past is to recognize how ancient cultures have contributed to today's world. The ideas and inventions that they developed have made our lives that much easier. More important, these ideas and inventions provide us with a foundation for improving the world for future generations.

The Olympic Torch

In ancient Greece, relay races with torches were held after dark. Today the Olympic torch is carried in a relay from Olympia, Greece, to the host city of the Olympic Games.

Power and Government

A philosopher called George Santayana once wrote, "Those who cannot remember the past are condemned to repeat it." Santayana's quote suggests that by learning about events of the past, we can avoid mistakes in the future. We may even find solutions to problems and improve our lives as a result. Bear this idea in mind as you examine important events in government.

Leaders from African nations gathered to discuss economic and political issues at an Organization of African Unity summit in 2000.

Building an Empire

Throughout history, there have been countries that have started out small but have become superpowers or empires. Most often, these empires declined or vanished over time. What lessons can we learn from this cycle of growth, power and decline? Let's look at some examples of empires and see what happened.

By AD 750 the Arabs had conquered lands stretching from Spain to India, creating a massive empire.

The Roman Empire

According to legend, Rome was founded in 753 BC as a tiny village of shepherds in central Italy. Over the next thousand years, its leaders steadily gained control over half of Europe, most of the Middle East and North Africa. Rome's reign was so widespread, that the emperor Augustus declared he had brought the "whole world under the rule of the Roman people".

Ancient Rome won land through a long series of battles and conquests. At one point, about 70 million people were ruled by the Romans. However, only one million lived in Rome itself. The rest lived elsewhere in Europe, the Middle East and Africa. These people did not share the same culture, language, customs or religious beliefs. Rather, the Roman emperors held them together with a strong system of laws.

Augustus, first emperor of Rome

However, the empire's territories simply grew too large to control. There were not enough soldiers to enforce the laws or protect the empire. This left it open to outside invaders from northern and eastern Europe. The western part of the empire finally collapsed in AD 476.

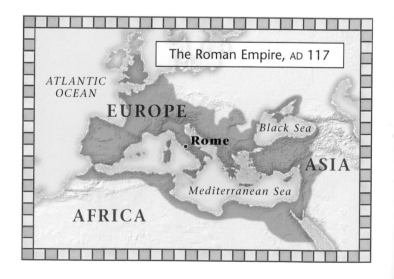

The Roman Empire, AD 117

ATLANTIC OCEAN

EUROPE

Rome

Black Sea

ASIA

Mediterranean Sea

AFRICA

The British Empire

By 1900 the British empire included about
a quarter of all the world's land. Wealth
poured into Britain from its many colonies
in Africa, Asia and Australia. By 1945, after
World War II, nationalism was a growing
force. The colonies wanted to be free and
independent nations. By 1970 most British
colonies had achieved that freedom.

India was a British colony until 1947.

Hitler's Conquests

Adolf Hitler came to power in Germany in 1933. Hitler and
his Nazi party promised to return Germany to a position of
power and glory after a crushing defeat in World War I. His
desire to build what he believed would be a perfect empire
led to tragedy and war.

Hitler claimed that Jews and many other groups were the enemy.

He planned to exterminate people who
didn't meet his idea of a perfect race. His
attempt to destroy all Jews is referred to as
the Holocaust. Hitler also murdered many
Russians, Poles, Gypsies, Slavs and Catholics.

In 1938 Hitler set out on his conquest
of Europe. He took over Austria and Poland
within a year. Next came the Netherlands,
Luxembourg, Belgium and France. Great Britain,
Australia, New Zealand, Canada, Russia and
the United States fought to defeat Hitler.
By 1945 Hitler was defeated. On 7th May
1945 Germany surrendered.

parade of the Nazi
armed forces

Alliances Among Nations

Today the world has no true empires. Taking over lands through conquest and ruling people from afar failed. History has shown us that the trend is towards smaller, independent nations. However, nations still join together in alliances. An alliance is a group of nations that forms for a purpose, such as trade or military strength.

An example from ancient history is the alliance between Sparta and Athens. In 500 BC, Sparta had a superior army and Athens had the strongest navy. Together, these Greek city-states formed an alliance to fight the Greeks' greatest enemy – the Persians.

Today, the United Nations, or the UN, is the largest alliance in the world. The UN peacekeeping forces, made up of soldiers supplied by member nations, serve in trouble spots around the world. The goal is to settle disputes. Think about what the world might be like if there was no such alliance to keep the peace.

a 6th-century BC bronze statue of a Spartan soldier

Soldiers wear blue berets when representing the UN. The UN headquarters is in New York City, United States.

History has shown us that strong trading partners are more likely to cooperate with one another. Moreover, trading with other nations is an important way to maintain a healthy economy. These are two reasons why trading alliances have existed throughout history.

During the Middle Ages an important trade region was located in northern Europe, around the Baltic and North Seas. In the mid-1100s groups of merchants that traded in this region formed the Hanseatic League. This alliance was created to protect the members from pirate attacks and foreign competition. By the 1200s more than seventy members had joined the alliance.

Today there are many trade alliances among nations. The European Union was formed in 1957. It includes many nations all over Europe. The European Union encourages trade and safeguards the rights of people living in member nations. The Commonwealth is a group of fifty-four nations. Many of these nations used to be part of the British Empire. The countries meet every two years to discuss ideas and ways to work together.

In 2002 twelve nations in the European Union adopted a common currency called the Euro.

Camels were used to carry goods along the Silk Road.

A Dangerous Route

The ancient Chinese traded goods with European merchants along the Silk Road. Goods such as silk were valuable, so it was a dangerous path to travel. Traders had to pay bribes to travel safely. Even so, bandits often robbed them along the way.

Struggles for Freedom

Imagine what your life would be like if you had no freedom. What if someone else told you they owned you and made you work for them without pay? People throughout history have struggled with the idea of slavery.

Many ancient Egyptian slaves came from the neighbouring country of Nubia.

From the earliest civilizations, slaves have been used as workers. The ancient Greeks, Romans and Egyptians used slaves to build palaces, to dig ditches and to work in their homes. Slaves had no rights. They could not refuse to work and they could not demand to be paid.

In the 16th century Europeans settled in North America. They needed strong, healthy men to build houses and to farm the land in these colonies. They also wanted to find new products to trade. The Europeans discovered that colonists would buy slaves to work the land, and the African slave trade began. Africans, many of whom had been warriors and tribal chiefs, were forced onto ships against their will and sold into slavery.

slave deck of a Spanish slave ship, around 1840

Democracy and Slavery

Is it right to own other people? Is it right to force them to work without pay? The moral issue of slavery has been debated almost as long as slavery has existed. The ancient Greeks had established a new type of government called democracy which means "rule by the people" in Greek. Democracy gave every Greek male citizen the right to voice his opinion, attend public meetings and elect political leaders. Despite their democratic ideas, however, the Greeks allowed slavery to be practiced.

Solon passed new laws in ancient Greece to promote democratic ideals.

Today, slavery has largely been made illegal. By looking at the evils of slavery and the many struggles for freedom, we can understand that the desire to be free is one that people share. It has helped us to understand the basic human rights of all people, whatever their race. Everyone has the right to be free, to have food and water, to have shelter, to worship or practise a chosen religion, to have their opinions and to be part of a wider community.

In many countries today people are able to openly voice their opinions.

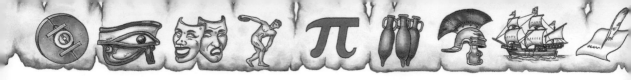

Linking the Past and Future

Nearly every important development in modern times can be linked in some ways to events in ancient history. This book has covered just some of these developments. Many other aspects of our lives that we take for granted have their roots in ancient civilizations. As you think about life and events happening around you, think about how the past has led to the ideas and actions of our time. Think about how past mistakes have been corrected to make a better world. Also, think about how your knowledge of the past can help provide ideas for the future.

Recommended Reading

Ancient China
Anita Ganeri, London:
Belitha Press, 2003

Ancient Greece
Anne Pearson, London:
Dorling Kindersley, 1997

Ancient Greece Revealed
Peter Chrisp, London:
Dorling Kindersley, 2003

Eyewitness Books: China
Arthur Cotterell, London:
Dorling Kindersley, 2000

Eyewitness Books: Explorer
Rupert Matthews, London:
Dorling Kindersley, 2003

*Eyewitness Books:
North American Indian*
David Murdoch, London:
Dorling Kindersley, 2000

Eyewitness Books: Viking
Susan Margeson, London:
Dorling Kindersley, 2002

A Journey Through Time
Richard Bonson, London:
Dorling Kindersley, 2001

The Original Olympics
Stewart Ross, London:
Hodder Wayland, 1999

*People of the World:
Population and Migration*
Brian J Knapp, Henley on
Thames: Atlantic Europe
Publishing, 1994

*The Usborne Internet-Linked
Encyclopedia of World History*
Fiona Chandler, London:
Usborne, 2002

*Wow: Discoveries, Inventions,
Ideas and Events That
Changed the World*
Philip Ardagh, London,
Macmillan Children's
Books, 2002

Index